Labradoodles

by Ruth Owen

PowerKiDS
press™

New York

Published in 2013 by The Rosen Publishing Group, Inc.
29 East 21st Street, New York, NY 10010

First Edition

Produced for Rosen by Ruby Tuesday Books Ltd
Editor for Ruby Tuesday Books Ltd: Mark J. Sachner
US Editor: Sara Antill
Designer: Emma Randall

Photo Credits:
Cover, 1, 3, 4–5, 6–7, 8–9, 10–11, 12–13, 15 (top), 16–17 (bottom), 18–19,
20, 24, 27, 30 © Shutterstock; 14–15 © FLPA; 17 (top) © Wikipedia Creative
Commons (public domain); 23 © Guide Dogs of the Desert; 25 © Ed Walthaus;
29 © Rob Louth www.reptilelife.co.uk.

Library of Congress Cataloging-in-Publication Data

Owen, Ruth, 1967–
 Labradoodles / by Ruth Owen. — 1st ed.
     p. cm. — (Designer dogs)
 Includes index.
 ISBN 978-1-4488-7857-4 (library binding) — ISBN 978-1-4488-7910-6 (pbk.)
— ISBN 978-1-4488-7916-8 (6-pack)
1. Labradoodle—Juvenile literature. I. Title.
 SF429.L29O94 2013
 636.72'8—dc23
                                    2011052874

Manufactured in the United States of America

CPSIA Compliance Information: Batch #B1S12PK: For Further Information contact Rosen Publishing, New York, New York at 1-800-237-9932

Contents

woof

Meet a Labradoodle!

What has a curly coat, loves to swim, and is very smart? The answer is a labradoodle.

Labradoodles are a **crossbreed** dog. This means they are a mixture of two different dog **breeds**, or types. When a Labrador retriever and a poodle have puppies together, they make labradoodles!

Most labradoodles are pet dogs, but some have been trained to work as **assistance dogs**.

Adult poodle

Adult Labrador retriever

Labradoodle puppy

An adult labradoodle

Want to know more about labradoodles? Keep turning the pages, and find out why so many people love "Doods"!

The First Labradoodle

Australian **guide dog** breeder Wally Conran was the first person to breed a labradoodle. In 1989, a woman named Pat contacted Wally. Pat was blind, and she needed a guide dog. Her husband had an **allergy** to dog hair, however.

Wally knew that Labrador retrievers make good guide dogs. He also knew that poodles have different hair than other dogs. Poodle hair does not bother people with allergies. Wally mated a Labrador retriever with a poodle, and they had labradoodle puppies.

The puppies' fur did not make Pat's husband sick. So one of the labradoodles was trained to be Pat's guide dog!

Labradoodle puppies

A five-month-old labradoodle puppy

The first labradoodle puppies that Wally bred were named Sultan, Sheik, and Simon. Sultan became Pat's guide dog.

Meet the Parents: Labrador Retrievers

Labrador retrievers are popular as pets. They were first bred to be working dogs, though. Their **ancestors** worked with fishermen in Newfoundland, Canada. The dogs would swim in the ocean and pull fishing nets to shore!

Today, some Labradors work as gun dogs. When a hunter shoots a bird or other small animal, the dog retrieves it and brings it back to the hunter.

Labrador retriever hair colors

Black   Yellow   Chocolate

A Labrador's mouth is so gentle that it can carry an egg without breaking it.

A working chocolate Labrador retrieving a duck

9

Meet the Parents: Poodles

Poodles are intelligent dogs that like learning new things. They were first bred to work with hunters, retrieving ducks and other birds from water.

Poodles have woolly, curly hair, and they come in different sizes. The biggest, the standard poodle, can measure 15 inches (38 cm) to the shoulder. The tiny teacup poodle may weigh only 2 pounds (900 g)!

A two-month-old poodle puppy

A standard poodle

Poodles are very good swimmers. The word poodle comes from the German word "pudel," which means "splashing in water."

Labradoodle Looks

Labradoodles often look like curly-haired teddy bears! Their hair color can be cream, apricot, gold, red, black, chocolate, and even silvery-blue.

Labradoodles get their curly coats from their poodle parents. Some labradoodles have tight, woolly curls like sheep's wool. Others have longer, wavy ringlets. A labradoodle's coat is water-resistant. This means that water runs off the hair instead of soaking through to the dog's body.

Adult labradoodle size

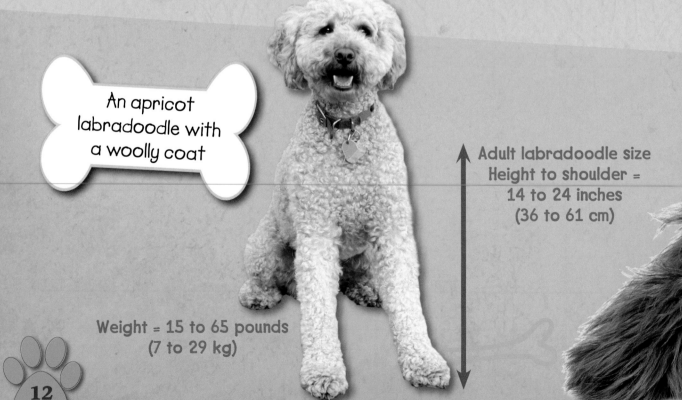

An apricot labradoodle with a woolly coat

Adult labradoodle size
Height to shoulder =
14 to 24 inches
(36 to 61 cm)

Weight = 15 to 65 pounds
(7 to 29 kg)

Labradoodle hair is safe for owners with dog-hair allergies. Also, unlike most dogs, labradoodles don't shed, or lose, their hair around the house!

A chocolate labradoodle with a wavy coat

Pups with Personality

Labradoodles are very clever dogs with lots of energy. When they are not on a leash, they clown around and have lots of fun. When they are on a leash or being trained, they are quiet and gentle.

Labradoodles are very friendly to new people and to other dogs. They are also very good at understanding their owners' moods and needs. This makes them good assistance dogs.

Labradoodles will play for hours, and they love to be in water. In fact, it's difficult to keep them out of water!

Oodles of Cute!

Some labradoodle puppies have a Labrador mom. Others have a poodle mom. The mother dog usually gives birth to about eight puppies in a **litter**.

When the puppies are first born, their eyes are closed. The tiny newborn pups drink milk from their mom and sleep. After about a week, the puppies' eyes open.

When the little pups are about four weeks old, they will be able to walk, run, and play!

The labradoodle puppies in a litter can be a mixture of different colors.

A newborn
labradoodle puppy

Nine-week-old
labradoodle puppies

17

Pet Doodles

Most labradoodle owners buy their puppy from a breeder. They visit a breeder and choose a puppy from a litter. When the puppy is ten weeks old, it can go to live with its new human family.

Pet labradoodles enjoy walks on the leash and time to run free in a backyard. They love to join their people hiking, running, and swimming.

A new member of the family

Labradoodle owners should brush their dog about once a week. If a doodle gets muddy, it's time for a bath with doggie shampoo!

Labradoodles love activities such as hiking.

A Very Important Puppy

Smart labradoodles enjoy working and pleasing their people. That's why they make good guide dogs.

If a labradoodle puppy is confident and pays attention to people, it might be chosen to become a guide dog. At eight weeks old, the puppy will go to live with a **puppy raiser**. The puppy learns commands such as "sit" and "stay." It visits busy, noisy places such as shopping malls.

If the puppy stays calm, follows commands, and works hard, it may be chosen to go onto guide dog training.

A Labrador guide dog

Guide dogs have to like people. When they are working, however, they cannot play or expect to be petted by strangers. A guide dog must focus on its work.

A labradoodle puppy training with her puppy raiser

Guide Dog Training

If a young dog is right for guide dog work, it starts training at 18 months old.

A guide dog must learn to stop at roadside curbs and at the top and bottom of stairs. It must be confident leading its owner onto buses and trains. It must also lie quietly while its owner is at work.

Being a guide dog is a labradoodle's perfect job. It gets to visit many interesting places and has a busy life.

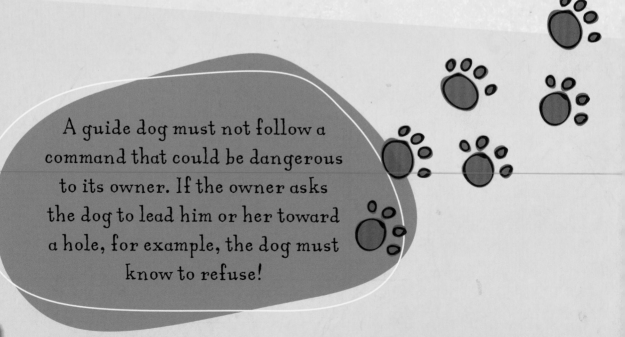

A guide dog must not follow a command that could be dangerous to its owner. If the owner asks the dog to lead him or her toward a hole, for example, the dog must know to refuse!

Victory, the labradoodle guide dog, and his owner, Ayia

23

Labradoodles Love to Help!

Labradoodles can be trained as therapy and service dogs. Therapy dogs give love and comfort to people in trouble. They visit people who are sick in the hospital. They spend time with children who have had sad things happen in their lives.

Service dogs work with people who need to use wheelchairs or have other disabilities. The dogs open doors, turn lights on and off, and pick up objects that their owners drop.

A therapy dog labradoodle

A service dog labradoodle

Therapy dogs sometimes visit disaster areas. If people have lost their homes in a hurricane or flood, they will be very unhappy. A wagging tail and friendly lick can bring lots of comfort!

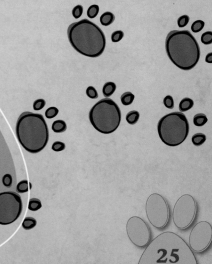

Smart Sniffs

Pearl is a labradoodle whose sense of smell can save her owner's life! Pearl's owner has diabetes. This means the amount of sugar in her blood can be too high or too low. When her blood sugar drops suddenly, she may get very ill. She could even die.

Pearl can smell when her owner's blood sugar is dropping. She warns her owner by touching her with her paws. Pearl will even fetch the telephone so her owner can call 911!

Drinking sweet juice helps diabetic people when their blood sugar drops. When Pearl's owner gets sick, Pearl fetches her a carton of juice from the refrigerator!

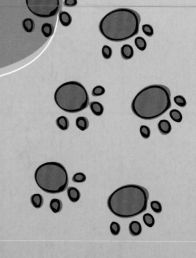

A nose that knows
how to help!

A Meerkat's Best Friend is a Labradoodle

In the United Kingdom, a lonely meerkat has become best friends with a labradoodle named George!

Disa, the meerkat, and George belong to Rob Louth. Rob keeps many animals including snakes, lizards, and tarantulas. Rob visits schools and gives show-and-tell talks about wild animals.

When Disa's meerkat partner Nicosi died, she was lonely and unhappy. Then one day she cuddled up to George's curly belly and went to sleep. Now the labradoodle and the meerkat are best friends!

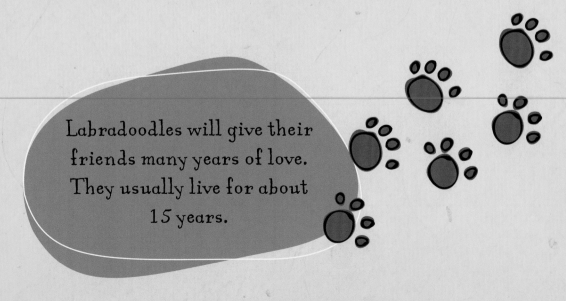

Labradoodles will give their friends many years of love. They usually live for about 15 years.

George the labradoodle
and Disa the meerkat

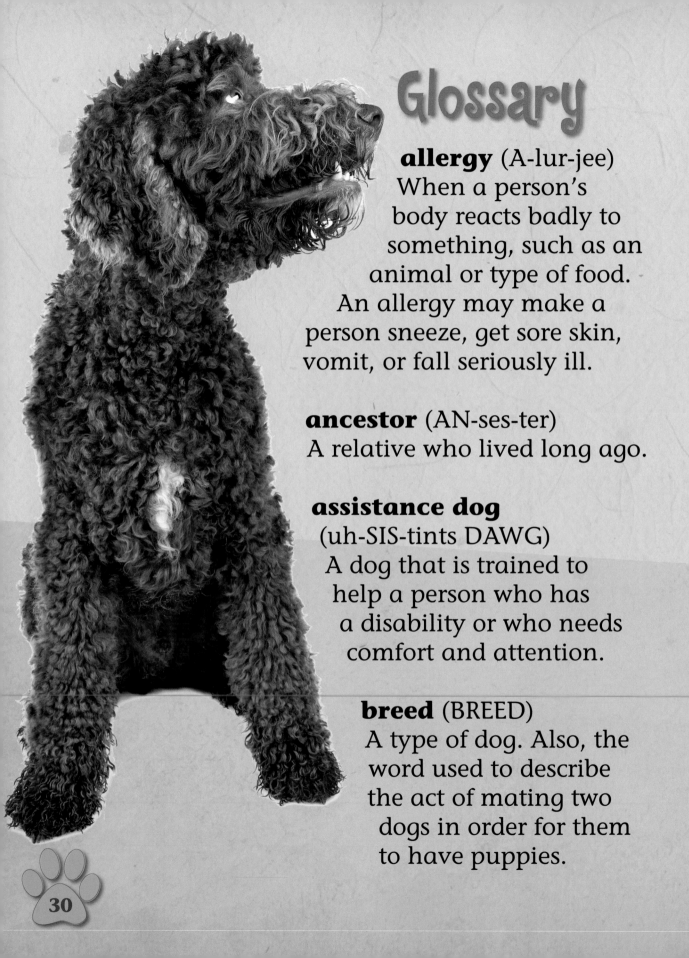

Glossary

allergy (A-lur-jee)
When a person's body reacts badly to something, such as an animal or type of food. An allergy may make a person sneeze, get sore skin, vomit, or fall seriously ill.

ancestor (AN-ses-ter)
A relative who lived long ago.

assistance dog (uh-SIS-tints DAWG)
A dog that is trained to help a person who has a disability or who needs comfort and attention.

breed (BREED)
A type of dog. Also, the word used to describe the act of mating two dogs in order for them to have puppies.

crossbreed (KROS-breed)
A type of dog created from two different breeds.

guide dog (GYD DAWG)
A dog that is trained to lead and protect a person who is blind or has difficulty seeing.

litter (LIH-ter)
A group of baby animals all born to the same mother at the same time.

puppy raiser (PUH-pee RAY-zer)
A person who cares for and helps to train a puppy that has been chosen to be a guide dog. The dog lives with the puppy raiser for about 18 months.

Websites

Due to the changing nature of Internet links, PowerKids Press has developed an online list of websites related to the subject of this book. This site is updated regularly. Please use this link to access the list:

www.powerkidslinks.com/ddog/labra/

Read More

George, Charles, and Linda George. *Labrador Retriever.* Top Dogs. New York: Scholastic, 2010.

Larrew, Brekka Hervey. *Labradoodles.* All About Dogs. Mankato, MN: Capstone Press, 2009.

MacAulay, Kelley, and Bobbie Kalman. *Poodles.* Pet Care. New York: Crabtree Publishing, 2007.

Index